From Hoodlums to Servants:

Fathering the Streets Gods Way

Devotional

Chicago Garfield Long

Library of Congress Catalog Number 2016917290
Published by
Vision House Publishers
Upper Marlboro, Maryland 20774
www.visionhousepublishers.com
support@visionhousepublishers.com

Table of Contents

- This Devotional Consist of 120 Subjects
- Each word has its definition
- Each word has a foot note for intent and application
- This devotional is geared toward all men
- Anyone raising or mentoring young males can benefit
- All 120 subjects are divided into 5 categories
- Man walking with **GOD , 24 Subjects**
- Man loving his **Woman, 24 Subjects**
- Man connecting with his **Children, 24 Subjects**
- Man strengthening **Himself, 24 Subjects**
- Man dealing with the **World, 24 Subjects**

Introduction

This book is dedicated to every male, especially the fatherless. This is a devotional, its power packed with daily spiritual and logical guidance for men. The intent of it is to sharpen your responsive actions in a godly manner and to bridge a stronger relationship between man and God. Its daily encouragement will surely build up your inner man and give you a greater thirst for God and building a faith centered loving family. Let it be known that Jesus Christ is the primary solution to correcting problems, aligning us on the proper paths and simply looking to him as our total source and resource for all good and perfect things. My Prayer is that by the dissecting of these words and their meanings, this devotional experience will release you from the bondage of pride, timidity, insecurity, fear of failure and the you in you that so often holds you back, push people away and destroy opportunities to unleash the greatness inside of you. Humble yourself where need be and allow it to help you to stand and take responsibility for your destiny, your actions, your relationships, the great need inside the community, your unbalanced emotions and to completely aid you into becoming all that God created us men to be.

Ephesians 3.20 *Now unto him that is able to do exceeding abundantly above all that you can ask or think, according to the power that worketh in us, to him   be   glory   and   majesty   forever.*

Concerning God

- *Warfare*
- *Sanctification*
- *Consecration*
- *Trust*
- *Believing*
- *Worship*
- *Faithful*
- *Grace*
- *Wisdom*
- *Understanding*
- *Truth*
- *Gift*
- *Control*
- *Discernment*
- *Silence*
- *Following*
- *Humility*
- *Long Suffering*
- *Planning*
- *Order*
- *Power*
- *Jesus*
- *Rest*
- *Anoint*

Concerning Self

- *Love*
- *Fasting*
- *Balance*
- *Savings*
- *Faith*
- *Study*
- *Discipline*
- *Exercise*
- *Pride*
- *Servant*
- *Self Control*
- *Consistency*
- *Prayer*
- *Atmosphere*
- *Strength*
- *Fathering*
- *Forgiving*
- *Accountability*
- *Responsibility*
- *Aggression*
- *Light*
- *Promise*
- *Dominion*
- *Support*

Concerning Women

- *Cover*
- *Protect*
- *Emotions*
- *Deposit*
- *Eating*
- *Authority*
- *Delegate*
- *Listening*
- *Dating*
- *Intimacy*
- *Patience*
- *Ministering*
- *Reputation*
- *Meekness*
- *Controlling*
- *Vision*
- *Communication*
- *Quality Time*
- *Respect*
- *Manipulation*
- *Observation*
- *Intercession*
- *Blessed*
- *Redeemed*

Concerning Kids

- *Provide*
- *Teach*
- *Inheritance*
- *Training*
- *Family Time*
- *Team*
- *Bonding*
- *Confidence*
- *Peace*
- *Persistence*
- *Discipline*
- *Disciple*
- *Leadership*
- *Affirmation*
- *Affliction*
- *Righteousness*
- *War*
- *Seeds*
- *Gratitude*
- *Appreciation*
- *Sin*
- *Christian*
- *Progress*
- *Impact*

Concerning World

- *Mentor*
- *Transparency*
- *Lust*
- *Hope*
- *Giving*
- *Lying*
- *Laboring*
- *Excellence*
- *Obedience*
- *Friendship*
- *Integrity*
- *Betrayal*
- *Community*
- *Money*
- *Deception*
- *Serpent*
- *Expose*
- *Fear*
- *Evil*
- *Curse*
- *Favor*
- *Distraction*
- *Gods Armor*
- *Bible*

- *A charge to the Men*
- *To the Youth*
- *To the Fatherless*
- *To the Single Mother*
- *To the Rejected/Black-Sheep's*

<u>*Concerning*</u>

<u>*God*</u>

<u>Warfare</u>

Definition

- *The waging of war, struggle and conflict physically or emotionally.*

    As Saints the weapons of our warfare are not carnal but mighty through God to the pulling down of strong holds.

    Pursue peace and rest in God, stand by faith knowing that he shall protect, perfect, provide and keep you out of harm's way, As you keep your mind stayed on him.

Sanctification

- *To set apart for sacred use, Consecrate, To make free from sin, Purify, To give religious sanction to, as with an oath, To give moral or social sanction to, To make productive of holiness or blessing.*

Sanctification is a necessary process that one must yield to in order to be changed from the old man into the new man that pleases God, Concerning carnal behaviors, responses and actions as a vessel to be used by God

Consecration

- *To initiate into order, To dedicate to a given goal or service, Dedication to sacred purposes, To set apart and to declare as holy and clean for the use of God.*

  This is a time used to esteem others for their faithful service and to entrust them with greater responsibility.
  It's a gathering for recognition for an honoree. This service can also be used to recommit an object inside the sanctuary or a religious dwelling place.

  Consecrating is a must and a necessary process before presenting yourself to be used as an instrument of God, in the home or the church. Apostle Paul states that it's his desire to decrease and for Gods spirit to increase when being used for service

14

Trust

- _Total confidence in the integrity, ability and good character of another, to commit to the care of another, Reliance on something in the future. Hope within something or someone._

  A needed response to God while on your Christian journey. Trust is a necessity when cultivating a relationship with others. Trust should be earned according to an individual's proven actions and responsive behaviors.

  There's a saying that goes you can't put your trust in one who will not trust you.

Believing

Definition

- To accept as true or real, to expect or suppose, A mindset to have or thinking, To have faith, esp. religious faith, to have a confidence in a truth, value or existence of something, To regard as true.

Believing is the vehicle that transports what you have faith for, or hope in, to come into a reality.

Scripture says that faith is the substance of things hoped for and the evidence of things not seen. Heb. 11.1 Also, without faith it is impossible to please God. Heb. 11.6 for we must first believe that God exists and that he is a rewarder to those that diligently seeks him.

Worship

Definition

- A set of religious forms, as ceremonies or prayers, by which love and honor is expressed. To honor, love and pursue a deity devotedly, in our case the Lord Christ Jesus, To participate in religious rites, to perform acts of reverence, To celebrate God and allow him to be seen through us, by his characteristics, being displayed through our lifestyle.

Faithful

Definition

- *Firmly and devotedly supportive, Loyal, worthy of trust or belief, reliable, consistent with truth or fact, having faith with a steadfast labor or action that supports ones belief.*

This is a requirement before taking on leadership or a level of responsibility. It's having a form of character that should be displayed under pressure or tempting to be declared as faithful. To be proven for consideration of exaltation from God. It is the proof of dependability.

Grace

Definition

- _To favor, to honor and enable, to impart. Divine love and protection bestowed freely on human beings, An excellence or power granted by God, A short prayer or thanksgiving said before or after a meal, An apparently effortless charm or beauty of movement, form or portion, A gift from God that declares and seals your redemption through Christ Jesus' shed blood on behalf of sin._

  Grace is an undeserved gift from God that's needed to grow and accomplish his will or purposes. It's because of his loving grace that we have redemption through the shed blood of Jesus, which presents us righteous before Gods Throne and free from the penalty of sin.

Wisdom

- *Understanding of what is true, right or lasting, Good judgment, Common sense, To be prudent and have discernment*

  Wisdom is a gift from God that ushers success in all your dealings with things that concern you. Wisdom is simply foreseeing good or demise in your near future.

  God is Omniscient, meaning all wise. He says in his Word that if any man lack wisdom, let him ask of him and he will give it freely without holding back. It's described as a gift in the book of James, the Word of Wisdom 1st Cor. 12

Understanding

- *The quality or state of one who understands or comprehends, Ones intelligence, An Individuals judgment or interpretation, An agreement or conclusion of two or more individuals or group, A reconciliation of differences in opinion, Agreement, Clear communication reached and declared, to move forward without hindrance, having good sense, comprehension and judgment of a matter*

Scripture says how can, two people walk together unless they agree. It begins with an understanding of morals, direction, plans and vision.

Truth

- *A fact or an actuality to be conformed to, Reality, A statement proven to be or accepted as true, Sincerity, integrity, Gods Written Word*

  Truth is the epitome of Gods Spoken Word and or the fact or reality of something we should adhere to.

  Truth is what God desires on the inward parts of Man.

Gift

Definition

- *Something bestowed voluntarily and without compensation, a talent, endowment, aptitude or a divine ability that edifies, exhorts comforts or entertains and brings good to the vessel and glory to God the giver.*

  God is looking for us to be faithful stewards over our gifts and talents, which he may multiply them and others may grow thereby. When we walk in our gifts they bring harmony to the atmosphere.

Control

- *To exercise authority or influence over, To direct, To verify or regulate, To hold in restraint, The ability to direct by influence*

  Taking control of one's self and all that concerns him is of great importance; however, attempting to control others without their agreement is degrading, immoral and selfish. Being controlling is a form of manipulation that stems from insecurities and is unhealthy for any relationship. God told us to take dominion over all the works of his hands, yet he did not say over each other. There must be honor and agreement.

Discernment

- *To perceive something hidden or obscure, to detect, to comprehend mentally and perceive differences.*

  Spiritually God will give us discernment of different spirits, personalities and phenomenon that surround us or that lingers in the atmosphere, in which we sometimes entertain unaware. Discernment is also considered a gift of the spirit and given as he the Holy Spirit wills and should be sought after at home, in the work place, public outings and church. Discernment is a form of protection from impending dangers or simple precaution. This gift occurs spontaneously. We should heed the scripture that says be slow to speak and swift to hear.

Silence

- *Refusing to give information or an opinion, Making no sound or noise, Secretive, Unable to speak, Unexpressed, The quality or state of being or the keeping of peace by silencing, Suppressed*

  Know when to hold your peace as husbands, sons, workers, offenders and ministers. This can save you from the bitter end of confusion, argument, loss of time, peace and things of value. Nothing wins someone over better than a great listener, who responds from a point of understanding the other. It takes our silence to grasp the out pouring, perception, ideas and creativity of the other to be successful in coming to an absolution and full proof plan.

Following

Definition

- *Adhering to the teachings or methods of another, a pursuer, an attendant, a servant or subordinate, to move or go along the course of something or someone.*

  It's wise to follow the teachings of Jesus Christ as a disciple. Likewise follow and obeying those that have rule over us in complete obedience for it pleases God and brings reward. Following leadership displays humility and one that has a teachable spirit. Opposite of Arrogance

Humility

- *The quality or condition of being humble, To be characterized by modesty or meekness in behavior, attitude or spirit, exhibiting submissive respect, Unpretentious, meaning undemanding or claiming position of distinction or Merritt when unjustified, nor puts on a show*

  God rewards the humble with exaltation, but he resists the proud. God is looking to see good character in operation in order to take us higher, for it's our good character that will sustain us there in.

Long Suffering

- *Patiently enduring or bearing wrongs and difficulties, Patient Endurance*

  Long Suffering is one of the fruits of Gods Character. The bible says that he is long suffering not willing that any should perish but come to repentance. This is a necessary fruit to bear when dealing with kids and the extremely difficult. A sign of maturity in a relationship with God, is knowing how to wait on him to move on our behalf

Planning

- *A detailed scheme or method worked out before hand for accomplishment of a project or special purpose, An outline or sketch as of a story to be acted out, A diagram of proposed intentions, To write down a vision or arrangement and to pursue it verbatim*

  Plain and Simple! You fail to plan you plan to fail. Put a process with those thoughts of creativity and dreams. Write it down and follow it to the letter, to ensure that there is order and a calculated success.

Order

- _A condition of order and logical arrangements among the individual elements of a group, A system, A systematic arrangement or design assembly for functioning and appearance, Prioritized in a sequential manner, A command given by a superior officer, a request for items, products, food or services._

  God functions in order not confusion. The bible says that Jesus isn't the Author of confusion. When there's order there's flow and a clearer picture of the desired goals. Scripture says to do things decently and in order

Power

- *The ability to act or perform effectively, A specific capacity, faculty or aptitude, strength or force exerted, Ability to exercise control over others, A person, A group or nation having influence or control over others*

Gods has given us a spirit of Power love and a sound mind. God has given us power over the enemy through the name of Jesus. In this earth realm we can speak things into existence; scripture says that there is death and life in the power of the tongue. We must walk in the Power of God's Word to be victorious.

Jesus

Definition

- *The founder and reason for Christianity, He's the Son of God, The sent Messiah, Prophet Priest King and Risen Lord of all who holds all Power and is seated on the right hand of the Father far above all spiritual wickedness, dominions and authorities in high places.*

  If you confess with your mouth that he is Lord and believe in your heart that God has raised him from the dead then thou will be saved. Romans 10. 9-10

Rest

- *The act of ceasing from work, activity or motion, quiet, ease, or refreshment from sleep or in activity, mental or emotional serenity.*

  It's simple to be at your best, your mind body and spirit needs to rest and be at peace or ease. Love yourself enough to make the time and feed your spirit Gods Word. The bible says to cast your cares on God for he cares for you. You can't be a blessing when you're drained and wired for hot all the time.

Anoint

- *A smearing on of ointment or oil with prayer that attracts the favor of God. Something designated by God and graced with a divine gift, to place oil on something as an indication of sanctification and consecration for ceremony and ordinance, a prayer of recovery by the laying on of hands and the asking for the absolution of sin.*

  To be anointed of God is to be sealed, endowed and approved by him. Anointing comes with season to be sent forth to function in the gifts of God. Without the anointing there is no super natural encounter or transfer for Gods Glory. The Anointing gives you divine access into the Spirit weather it's a gift that says, does or reveals. God shows, God speaks and God reveals.

Concerning

Self

Love

- *To have strong affection for someone based on experiences, attraction, sexual encounters or familial dwellings, an intense affection for someone or an object.*

- *Scripture says that love is kind, love is patient, Love Suffers Long, Love keeps no record of wrong doings, Love doesn't behave itself rudely, love doesn't seek her own and it's not puffed up, Love rejoices in the truth, love always hopes and trusts, Love protects, covers and it never fails*

  Most importantly understand that Love is an action word and it ceases to be love unless it's given out, otherwise its lip service. Secondly Gods love and if you're not being his hands and feet walking out and reaching out then you do not love.

Fasting

- _To abstain from certain foods, drinks or certain activities while giving yourself to prayer before God_
- _Fasting is a time of cleansing yourself for changed, empowerment and to be filled with the spirit of God_
- _Fasting gets Gods attention, although he is the same God all the time. Its yourself denial, obedience, seeking and worship that he delights in_

Balance

- *The means or power to decide, Emotional Stability, A harmonious arrangement of plans, elements and well being while multitasking or conducting other business requiring stressful decision making*

- *Balance is much needed; I would say it takes wisdom to find a life of balance. As a family man, trying to conduct business and work a full time job, my time for the kids recreation games in the evening, be ready on time for church service, date night with the wife, Gods time , me time and shopping. That's a lot of hats to wear without falling to sleep or failing. Your worst enemies are, negative energy, unhealthy eating, lack of sleep and being unprepared. You must take care of yourself and stick to your written vision for your life's work which brings you great fulfillment. Rescue yourself from stress and slaving over another man's vision. Be free in all that you do and think and you will find balance and harmony.*

Saving

Definition

- _Avoidance of over spending, To budget for the purposes of putting cash aside for specific reason, A reduction in penditure or cost, Preserving something of value._

  Weather your young, old, single, married or with kids. You must save for your future. You never know what shall come up. If your young and you desire to marry one day, prepare a place for your future Queen and kids.

  If you prepare a castle for your future queen its being wise. To be diligent is one thing, but to have a mind of preservation and self control for purposes of denying yourself pleasure for a period of time, for a beneficial future, comes with wisdom and experience. Surely this is a way of increasing the chances of peace, security for your woman, independence and strength/power.

  Don't be foolish to think that a rainy day will not come, for there will be many throughout life, as well as with family and friends that will experience them when you don't. Don't have a selfish mindset as a man, for we are providers by nature and If you're not positioning yourself to do so, you are void of understanding, yourself centered and lack the mindset of a strong husband and good loving father. Sometimes we weren't taught to have such strength and we just have to learn through experience and hardship.

Faith

Definition

- *The substance of things hoped for and the evidence of things not seen, it's a confident belief in the truth, value, or trust worthiness of a person, idea or a thing, Belief not based on logical proof or material evidence. Belief and trust in God*

Scripture says without faith it's impossible to please God. Heb 11...6
Our faith will accomplish what we send it to do when we line up with God's Word/Desires

Life can render some serious beat downs by circumstances and people and faith is the vehicle that in God is the vehicle that will bring you out victoriously every time.

Study
Definition

- *The act or process of studying, the pursuit of knowledge as, as by reading, observation, or, research, a work, a result from studious endeavor.*

Scripture tells us concerning the oracles of God, to study to show thy self approved as a workman that needs not to be ashamed but rightly dividing the Word of truth.

Scripture also indicates that it's not good to be without knowledge and knowledge makes a man's face to shine, in other words, in our walking in knowledge and the wisdom to apply it our very countenance will change. Knowledge is power. If you're in position to lead trust that you will have to feed them knowledge concerning your line of work.

Discipline

Definition

- *Training expected to yield a different type of pattern of behavior, Training that produces moral or mental improvement.*
- *Controlled behavior resulting from disciplinary training.*
- *Punishment intended to correct and train, Systematic method to obtain obedience, a state of order based on submission to authority.*

Without discipline our flesh will be all over the place and we would accomplish very little. Discipline precedes good integrity. Concerning the things of God our flesh wars daily with our Spirit, so there must be a discipline to engage God and deal with your own self weakness honestly without pride having its way.

Exercise

Definition

- *An activity requiring physical or mental exertion, when performed to maintain or develop fitness, something practiced so as to increase ones skill or strength.*

Long Live the King

They say the young and successful, the mid aged and passionate always arise early and strengthen themselves for the day, the battle and to outlast competition.

Exercise increases blood flow, to every part of your body and promotes anti aging, illness and disease. It's not an option, stay diligent and potent for your wife to keep those intimate times joyful for the both of you.

The same goes for your kids and being submitted for the use of Gods purposes, your health is vital for quality of life for self and those you protect and provide for. Appreciate good health by maintaining it.

Pride

Definition

- *A sense of one's own proper value or dignity, Self respect, an overly high opinion of oneself, one of the seven cardinal sins, to indulge in self esteem.*

  A self centered, selfish, arrogant and inordinate response to people and situations, Proud and haughty look
  God says he hates a proud look and a lying tongue. God is surely into us having a good attitude.

  We must not let pride get the best of us during the times we should let things run their courses and allow process to take place. At some point you must know that forms of fighting are just not profitable to you. When there is truth , like your betterment for instance, the situation may had been sent by God or allowed just to break you then rebuild you back up with greater strength and foundation. Nobody likes change, but it's necessary. God put you here for a purpose and it wasn't just for you only to enjoy everything but to be equipped to carry, help, pick up or bear the burdens of others that you so claim you love or that you support.

  Don't let pride destroy you and take everything and your love ones from you. God resist the proud but exalts the humble. Choose your battles wisely for though you may win it just may cost you the lives of others, not physical corruption death, but death by separation and loss of grace.

  Pride is about self and eventually leads and leaves you to yourself. *Quote by Chicago Long*

Servant

- *One expressing submission or debt to another, One that serves another even before him or herself, One that assist in aiding others to be of assistance or to promote interest.*

- *Jesus said who is greater among you except he who serves.*
- *Ones heart must be conditioned to be a servant otherwise you're just doing things for multiple reasons, some with good intentions and some with selfish motives attached. The proof is in the attitude of excellence or the complaint and murmur of lip service.*

Self Control

Definition

- An individual's control over his or her feelings, desires
  and actions by their own will.
  Self control is a fruit of the spirit. It's a necessary
  discipline to exemplify patience, love and inner peace.
  Its surely a sign of maturity, being shy and refraining
  from doing something, because of a fear of people will
  not suffice for having self control due to insecurity
  issues that give appearance as if, to refrain out of
  strength.

  Self control is revealed by test of pressure to maintain
  without deviation of planned routine or assignment
  It takes prayer and positive attitude to achieve the
  altitude necessary to hurdle imperfections and
  hindrances that cripple us and cause delay and fruitless
  labor.
  Coming to the realization that we can't control the
  uncontrollable will sustain us within Gods peace. You
  must believe God has all power in this instance

Consistency

Definition

- *Being conformed to the same course of actions or principals, holding a steady focus without waiver in your important dealings or that which concerns you.*

When a man is consistent it gives a woman great security, as well as in the bonding with children/youth. Consistency is a trait of an individual who possesses good character by way of experience, true sign of maturity that yields reward and good reputation. Scripture says that a diligent hand shall have much and a faithful man shall abound in blessings. Aligning yourself to being consistent is honorable.

Fathering

- *To Acknowledge responsibility for, A man who creates or originates something, To begat, To cover children or dependants with food, shelter, emotional support, a guidance, a counselor, and an example of survival strength and love.*

Father is the necessary main ingredient to raising a family. A child should have a father present in the home as an example or replica of heaven, Gods intention for replenishing the earth and carrying his title as Father. The Father is the one called to be head of house hold, the leader and initiator etcetera. Only a Father can tell a daughter what type of man is good for her and show a son how to be a man by example.

Forgiving

- *To excuse for a fault or offense, To pardon, To absolve from payment of what's owed*

He's the God of all comfort

Forgiving someone is not for them, but for you

- *Scripture says that if we don't forgive others of their trespasses against us, then our heavenly Father can't forgive us of our trespasses.*
If you want to experience relief, ease, peace and relaxation after a situation, then you must learn to lay aside every weight that burdens you, even so sin if need be. Letting go of something that you do understand or someone that hurt you is not always easy, especially when you can still feel the pain that it caused. You must have a trust in God, for he will replace, restore and see you through the situation at hand. Rendering evil for evil is not your job. The battle is not yours, but it's Gods, because he is the great judge and loves judgment. We are all human and subject to faults through misunderstandings, lack of communication, insecurities, fear, impatience, greed, immaturity and lust of the flesh which we have all fallen victim to, just from getting hurt alone. Yes! Hurt people do hurt people out of anger and a fear from being hurt again. Love covers a multitude of sins and it begins with a heart of forgiving. Don't be afraid to allow forgiveness and Gods healing hand of restoration to heal your broken relationships, God will reward you for trusting in him to fix it and allowing him to get the glory out of your life. It shows him that even though you have committed your heart to loving something or someone else you don't put them before him, but you commit all things to him for his blessing to be upon it. Do yourself and the world a favor by living your life to the fullest without the bitterness of past hurts, faults and failures. The sun will shine my brother, but Gods going to cause it to shine inside of your heart first, don't fight it. Start releasing before it makes you ill in every facet of your being and running over only to destroy what's left on the outside. Love is your weapon, stay on your face and in Gods face.

Accountability

Definition

- *Required to render account, to act in a creditable way, to yield yourself to being available or present to a person or group by schedule or request. A readiness to give explanation, expertise, provision, participation, performance, reason, report concerning business or solution.*

Without accountability no team can remain stable and without confusion. Accountability goes hand in hand with order and protocol and without this act of respect everything bonded together would fall apart. Everyone has an integral part to play and there's got to be a way of tallying results and suggestions for betterment even so complaint. It's the respected process of accountability that glues every element, individual, experiment, project, routine and blueprint etcetera together for success and unison.

I prescribe the prescription of accountability to the reckless and wild, particularly those that stay as an island off to themselves with no productivity. Some of us grow up never learning nor witnessing how to submit to authority. This is a major issue in the homes of the single mothers raising kids without a Father, and they come out with no balance confused and shocked by a worlds system that forces them out of their comfort zones and paralyzed to a truth never taught. Believe it or not sometimes these encounters combined with other issues and struggle can domino into mid life and early life crisis. Without a proper support system it can usher bad habit and sober less judgment. Teach accountability and submission to authority.

Responsibility

Definition

- *Something for which one is accountable, Being legally or ethically accountable for the welfare or care of another, making moral or rational or rational decisions on one's own, capable of being trusted and dependable, Having good judgment based on experience, Having the means to pay debts and meet obligations.*

Lead by example and be sure to put others through the test before entrusting your treasures and partnering up with them in any fashion/relationships of all kinds that require results based on performance

Aggression

Definition

- *Initiating forceful or hostile actions against another, To Attack, to violate ones space or territorial rights, the practice of encroaching, to be combative, to have bodily assertion.*

You must teach your family self defense for the streets and how to be competitive in the corporate arena. One will break them down physically and the other emotionally and financially. Teach them to defend themselves and hold their ground against bullying and how to defuse aggressive situations with wisdom and confidence.

Fathers be sure not to provoke nor instill the wrong attitude and spirit into your child while doing so. You wouldn't want them to become what you're teaching them to watch out for.

Light

Definition

- *A spiritual awareness, something that enlightens or provides information, Ones individual opinions, choices or standards. To signal, direct or guide with or as with lights. Illuminable*
- *The glorious light of the Gospel of Jesus the Christ*

Scripture says that you as sons of God you are the light of the world. Let your light so shine before men that they may see your good works and glorify the Father in heaven. It then asks a question should we hide such a great light under a bushel? It goes on to say that we should sit it up on a hill to be seen by all and to shine brightly.

Do me a favor, go into the bathroom and stand in front of the mirror, with all the lights out and tell me about your appearance... Well you can't because you're in darkness, it's the same way living without Christ you are surely in darkness and blinded to the things of God as you go about in your sinful nature and natural mindset. Its only when you look into the light of God's Word that you can see all your blemishes and the light now illuminates your dark areas and sinful nature that keeps you separated from the fellowship of God and Christ Jesus the hope of Glory and the light of men.
Scripture also says that in God there is no darkness and if we say we have fellowship with him and walk in the darkness we lie and the truth is not in us.

Promises

- *An assurance that one will or will not do something. To pledge or offer assurance to provide basis for expecting a future that's well.*

  He who promised is faithful said the Lord
  There are over 2000 promises in the Word of God
  claim them as an heir of God

  Do what you say you're going to do. Don't make an oath and not perform it.

Dominion

Definition

- *Supreme authority and control to dominate*

  God said to take dominion over all the works of his hands not each other

  Take dominion as a king on his throne. What kind of king will you be?
  How do you function as a Prince now?
  When the righteous are in rule the people rejoice.

Support

- *To carry the weight or burden of, to maintain in position so as to keep from falling, sinking or sleeping. To bear or withstand, to keep from falling or yield during stress/process, to provide for with money or necessity. To aid the case or cause by approving, favoring or advocating, To endure, Tolerate, To play a part or a role in someone's life or a situation*

Don't talk about it be about it. Love isn't love unless it given away.

God loves a cheerful giver and if you can't do it with joy then don't give it at all.

Everybody needs a support system, Everybody makes mistakes and have short comings, But the truth is when someone is in need, they're in need regardless of how they got their and if it's in your power to do good do it, as long as its beneficial to their bodies and spirit for nourishment shelter or betterment.

Concerning

Women

Cover

Definition

- *To hover over with the intent to conceal or protect and shield. To give support financially, emotionally and spiritually, To prevent from danger, damage, demise or enemies*

It sounds like nurturing or fathering someone to me. Scriptures tells that she's to leave and cleave to us, if you're to be Husband to her and take on the same attributes of a Father it's crucial that you can avail yourself to meeting the same needs as he does in addition to intimacy.

It is very important that a man be able to demonstrate that he can cover a daughter before marrying her, either on his own or with the necessary support system to ensure quality of life. You must understand exactly how your woman was brought up and how she was affected by her childhood relationships, otherwise you can't effectively minister to her needs or in her love language. Husbands love your wives as Christ loved the church by laying his life down for it.

Protect

Definition

- *To keep from harm, attack or injury, to guard.*

   It's a man's job to defend, stand guard and be watchful naturally, emotionally, spiritually, and financially
   A wise man knows to seek and trust God to be his total source and resource for all his needs.
   Always have a backup plan of provision if normal routine and current set budgets suffer compromise, it's a wise practice and it builds a strong foundation of trust and security with your woman. In doing so it would make her feel safe and confident to entrust you with her life and the lives of her kids, if it's a readymade family.
   Always keep a woman guessing concerning romance, charm and intimacy, but never concerning the direction you're leading her and the welfare of her kids, if they're under your roof and management.
   Men don't take a woman to yourself to wife, from under the provision of a good Father knowing her quality of life will change dramatically, you're asking for more than hardship. Trust me if your wife is not initiating talking and walking by faith, you have got to assure her in the natural first of her welfare, in addition to preaching a future into being by faith. Faith cometh by hearing and that's a process according to time spent in God's Word. Dwell with her according to knowledge and protect her from emotional panic, shock and break downs. When a woman feels safe, secure and wanted my dear boy! You have yet to experience bliss in every form and to the highest degree all because you manned up like a Father that covers a daughter and conducted yourself as a true son under God in your dealing righteously with her. She needs complete protection and this sort of haven keeps her home. Now golden nugget here dear boy! Should for any reason she give you ungratefulness in return after giving her provision as surety, Then you leave her right where you found her because she doesn't want you. It's tight, but its right, I speak of courting phase young Prince. A wise woman would know she's being treated as a Queen and should honor a King accordingly. A wise woman builds a house and a foolish one plucks it down. Don't volunteer for abuse and misuse.

Emotions

Definition

- *A state of agitation or disturbance, A complex response as to love or fears*
- *The part of the consciousness that involves feelings or sensibility*

God has designed women to bear so much emotionally and still keep ticking and being mothers, business women, ministers, wives and above all else best friends with multiple women. Not only are you to maintain and keep a cool head about you, but you've got to make sure that she's secured in every way.

Knowing your woman is vital, because they are all just like little girls with a daddy when they're with you, you got some that are monstrously prideful and independent, Miss I don't need nobody who never really had a daddy daughter relationship or had too much of it and are still under the cradling bond of an over protective loving dad. Understanding her stress points, weaknesses, times of frustration and where you need to get in to fit in, while giving her enough space to grow, collect her thoughts and evolve and have an opportunity to walk in her strengths is necessary. Bruh, it all starts with listening to her with the intent to take on a new job daily. Since she's ever changing you got to remain attentive and ready to minister to her constantly without being over bearing or a know it all. Many times women just act out and get spoiled and you surely better have balance in dealing with her, because some things don't change overnight and the last thing you want is to be in a relationship pulling in two different directions because you as the man can't identify her love language or when you need to stand firm and say something needs to change. Some woman have been abused and simply hiding her brokenness behind all that sexy she displays, but focus on Just being her best friend, above all her man of God, always keep him center of the relationship.

Deposit

Definition

- *To give as partial payment or security, To invest into an account or person/venture*

How is this relevant to a woman? In every way my dear boy! <u>*Don't expect to get a return or withdraw from your woman*</u> *<u>if there has been no deposit</u>. If you haven't planted seeds of love, sacrifice, quality time, serving, just because gifts, just being into her, gifts of silence and peace, and above all the seeds of righteousness don't get your hopes up, with a strong woman with good self esteem anyway.*

You must understand that a woman is an incubator and what you sow into her comes out magnified. You sow nothing and she just may not show up. Give her a house she will give you a home. Give her a bag of groceries and she will make a meal. You get it by now. Apart from that, your bank account Sir it says insufficient funds, this is not securing her emotionally concerning her future with you. Its situations like this that bring her doubt panic and cause her to hide money and being divided financially. Get out your comfort zone or insecurities and get on the grind. Launch something together and build a legacy.

A man must wash his woman with the Word of God to present her to himself. Deposit love, strength, trade skills and family tradition into your kids. Duplicate yourself.

Eating

Definition

- *To consume food, to feed yourself, to nourish your body.*

Good eating habits should be acquired for optimal health. Practice a good diet to avoid obesity disease and to look good and feel good, I meant all of that for your wife Sir! She wants you to look good and feel good during intimacy. If you can't love yourself how can you effectively love her? Don't be selfish, but ensure that you will be there for your kids wedding and grand kid's graduations. Don't make your wife feel like she's going to have to wheel Chair you around... Healthy eating breeds a positive mood, energy and vitality. Your wife wants a Super Man plain and simple. She will settle for Clark Kent while in the grocery store.

Following a good exercise regiment with strength training and healthy eating projects strength, promotes envy and is honorable.
Seriously, the Life of the body is in the blood so you are what you eat and drink. Detoxify often and do short fast while consuming lots of water. No Cancer thrives inside an oxygenated body. Stay hydrated with clean water. You must be prone to giving off positive energy in the atmosphere or home from healthy thinking. Loving thoughts thinketh not evil and hopeth in all things Feed your brain knowledge.

Authority

Definition

- *The right and power to enforce rules regulation and law,*
- *To determine Leadership delegation,*
- *Freedom or right to grant another authorization,*
- *Leadership*

Walk in your authority as a Man of God in your home, community and church.

Lead by example and perform your promises as spoken.

Taking authority over situations that need resolve puts at ease a loving wife.

Scripture says that God has given us the authority to bind and loose here in the earth realm. Matthew 16. 19 What so ever we bind on earth shall be bound by heaven and what so ever we loose on earth shall be loosed by heaven. We are the initiators of change.

If your woman has walls built up and she's always in a state of defense or to rebel then you may need to check your communication for nobody likes to be demanded to do anything. The woman came from your side, not under your foot; she's to stand beside you as an equal and help meet, as you lead her. Her place is one of meekness, that's power under control for though she can be just as strong, yet submissive. Sub means under and missive or mitt means mission, but if you as the man have no mission then how can she come under you? Effective communication is what you say and how you say it and your body language. You could be saying the right things but your attitude is degrading, self centered and unloving. Love your woman and accept her where she is and be willing to grow together as one and not apart. It's your job to feed her Gods Word. Meshing as one is a process that calls for a patient, strategic and purposeful harmonizing in every encounter? Touch her without touching her. Don't order her around; there is power in suggestion and leading. Don't force the fitting, be willing to die to your egotistical pride and self to win her over and your union will be fruitful and blessed, as you both follow the vision that God has given you as the visionary. She should trust your judgment.

Encourage

Definition

- *To inspire with hope, Courage or Confidence*
- *To give support, To Foster good ingredients for success and well being within another*
- *To impart strength during struggle, failure, hardships or weakness*
- *To cheer up and cheer on, To peek up*

Family and Good Friends Encourage You

In this life we sometimes get misunderstood by others or find ourselves afar off from support systems, even so finding ourselves divided from love ones due to misperceptions , mistakes and prideful attitudes. When it seems like you're on an island off to yourself and your discouraged and you can't see hope, you must look up to God and within yourself for strength. Learn to build yourself up daily and lean and depend on God to bring you to an expected end.

Having pity parties and remaining in a dark place only delays your day of sunshine. You must command your flesh to press its way into the rays of light or the open door to liberation. Stand on God's Word and holdfast to your confession of his promises that await you. My Pastor use to say it may be a fact that you don't have any money or a job but the truth is God shall supply your every need according to his riches and glory through and by Christ Jesus. Don't waste any more time on the hurt people caused you and the pain of your progression but focus your mind on the pressing into your break through and break out. Everything happens for a reason and God still holds all power and has everything in and under control at all times. Your body can't move forward without your mind, TAKE IT BACK! And be consumed by the things of God and his love. Many are the afflictions of the righteous but the Lord delivereth them out of the all. The name of the Lord is a strong tower and the righteous run into it and they are safe. M

Sometimes we can't be only where we are celebrated, thicken your skin and stand through the discouraging attacks and perceptions others give off.

Listening

Definition

- *To hold your peaces or cease from speaking while another speaks, To hear another out completely*
- *Preparation for counseling or reasoning,*
- *Entertaining another's views, opinions or side of a story*

Nothing beats a good listener when you need to vent and be understood on a matter. Apart from that how else can you come to agreement with another party?

It's been said time after time that behind every strong or successful man is a strong woman, well who ever this guy is he obviously listens to his woman , which means he involves her and shares with her and if he does that then he must trust her instincts and judgment. The problem is some of us men just won't bring or selves to drop the ego with our significant other and reason being you simply probably chose poorly when selecting a woman to commit to. So what do you do at that point? You must feed and lead and protect your investment. Get her educated and into the right atmospheres to improve quality of life and decision making. This way you two will not be divided and pulling in two different directions based on trust issues and a lack of communication given to selfish ambitions. If you got a great woman appreciate her and bring the best out in her by celebrating her and cultivating the relation bond with unhindered harmony from petty and childish murmurings. A wise man listens and increases in knowledge and he also keeps discretion. Stop shooting down every idea and suggestion she has, along with your, I know everything attitude, It's discouraging and ungrateful to be responded to be the person you love and are trying to help. Walk as one and conquer together.

Dating

Definition

- *An appointment time to go out socially with another person to an engagement. A marked time for a specific moment.*

Dating plays a major role initially in the beginning of a relationship as well as during the apex of married life. Dating keeps the romance and bonding times strong, it's a time to stalk that fire, experience new things together and communicate and connect even stronger emotionally. Dating is a very intimate time and it's a form of love language and a place to fulfill all the rest, for example quality time, giving gifts, affection, words of affirmation and other encouraging jesters that says I'm here to stay I want you more than I did yesterday.

Intimacy

Definition

- *In – 2- ME-C*
- *To communicate by any means necessary with the intent to be affectionate with expression, touching, caressing, love making, charming, holding, listening, participating in activities of equal enjoyment or with the intent to sacrifice or support another, eye gazing and holding hands.*
- *Letter Writing*

This is what floats her boat my dear boy! And it starts with that gentle nudging or embrace when turning over to say good morning. A note next to the coffee before work that says I love you and daddy got something special planned after dinner this evening, Maybe just simply falling on your face in prayer on her side of the bed and laying hands on her to transfer blessing. There are millions more.

If you don't know by now its two things that causes climax with a woman and the first is emotional stimulation, then her spots in many areas of her body, most importantly that deep penetration, that hits rock bottom. All women differ, be it bodily or emotional need and it's your job to minister to it in the proper sequence, but for the most part they all have similarities. Keeping your body in great shape and eating right increases blood flow to the male sex organ, ensuring longevity and pleasure for great intimacy with your wife.

Trust me many marriages fail because of 3major things and that's lack of money, unpleasurable sex and bad communication, its possible for one to affect them all, so this is very necessary to address Sir! If you aren't talking right, listening right and money is not right, it's possible for your woman to shut down and be detached even while in sexual acts. We must man up around the board to keep our woman feeling safe and secure.

Intimacy is the lifeline of any relationship with a woman; she thrives on it and thinks about it day and night, especially when out of your presence. Making contact with her person is vital and showing concern for what going on with her opens the door to questions and answers, which gives you a cheat sheet for giving her support and comfort. She will tell you what she wants if you ask her.

Keep God centered in it just because he's your total source and resource. Please forgive me for my straight forward delivery of truth.

Patience

Definition

- *The capacity of calm endurance*
- *Capability to endure affliction calmly,*
- *Tolerant and Understanding, Persevering*
- *Able to bear delay*
- *One who suffers lack with a held hope/expectation*

Patience is one of the nine facets of the fruit of the Spirit
It's a vital attribute for leaders, parents, relational partners and business investors

As husbands we must be patient with our wives and children. Meshing with readymade families, multiple personalities, day to day routines and marriage bonding can wear us out, causing us to become short with one another.

Scripture says let Patience have her perfect work in you that you may be complete and entire wanting nothing.

<u>Ministering</u>

<u>Definition</u>

- *Performing religious functions in church settings or home, To serve, To attend to the needs and wants of others, To administer*

Faith Love and Hope

All Ministry starts at home with the family or with yourself. You must bring home in order first, before trying to fix the house of God. They say Happy Wife, Happy Life, as you see ministering means serving. First understand that you are the Priest of your home, so there's a demand on leading by example for you concerning your being a teacher of the oracles of God. Just Keep it simple and sweet and meet her needs. Loving your wife as Christ loved the church is a command directed to husbands. You must be the example you want to see in her.

Remembering home is the first line of business when it comes to ministering. Teach her how to love you the by the way your loving her.

Reputation

Definition

- *A specific characteristic or trait attributed to someone.*
- *A good or bad report of someone's proven behavior*
- *A state or situation being held in high repute*

Reputation denotes your past or current stand even so, what you walk in. It's also a clear report of your integrity. A good reputation is to be desired over great riches. Has your reputation been destroyed? Have you been lied on before? Have you been oppressed intentionally or pressured to be something you're not? Better yet, have you just messed everything up on your own and everything is simply true about how you're viewed? Well you have two options here, you can let it break you and crawl in your angry hole or you can decide to chuck it up , forgive yourself and others and just change, with a mindset that you're going to walk in the vision God gave you. Trust me, it's very hard to swallow, because after such hardships, failures and mistakes it makes you want to through in the towel or play the blame game. My brother, just take it one day at a time no matter where you find yourself. You must put your faith in Jesus the Hope of Glory. Sometimes your daily fight is on the battlefield in your own mind. Tell yourself God is not finished with you and what others think doesn't matter a hill of beans ANY LONGER! And that's just it; you're being moved by the multitude that's fickle and subject to change weather your doing good or bad. People will always formulate judgment and opinion without a helping hand and leaving you to yourself including dyer situations, simply underestimating you and counting you out. Keep believing! Your faith is sometimes all that you have, when feeling secluded in a dark place of discouragement. Look within yourself and to God whose strength is made perfect in our weaknesses for help. God knows, Sees, hears and most certainly cares for you. This too shall pass; put your feet to your faith, for there's no other way to please HIM other than your obedience and unshakable and unbreakable faith. Assure yourself daily that you are the apple of Gods eye and you and him are the majority, for he will make a way out of no way. Don't faint and don't leave him for he will neither leave you nor forsake you. Keep your eyes off the current and keep them on the Lord who is your help and comforter in the time of need. Call on him!

Meekness

- *Power under control, Exemplifying patience, humility and gentleness*
- *Being submissive while full of strength*

Sometimes instead of telling others, you simply have to keep calm and say to self that meek doesn't mean weak and rise above petty, arrogant, foolish and jealous trouble makers. Some people call them haters my dear Boy! Be at peace and wise enough to foresee that sometimes holding your peace and walking away counts as a win. We all will reap a harvest from what we sow Let go and let God

You're probably right! They don't want any parts of you nor could they stand to be called out and exposed on their foolishness and short comings. Neither is it Gods desire for us to go ahead of him to choose a path of destruction.

Now concerning your woman, GET IT TOGETHER! Who do you think you're talking to? We as men need to learn that our wolfing with our women doesn't make things change for the better all the time and certainly not immediately. Hear her out and learn to reason with a tone that is respectable. Never try to intimidate or over power your woman save that for love making, but with compassion. You want to make her better not worst or the same. Control your temper.

Proverbs 15. 1 says a soft answer turns away wrath.

If you listen right without cutting her off and acting like you know everything, I guarantee you she will not have to raise her voice and she won't have her back turned at bed time either. Never argue before sleep or discuss major issues.
Pillow talk it into her heart, while you hold her in your arms. This goes a long way with a woman that loves you. You will surely get a much better responding woman who has learned to keep her power under control, based on your example through love. Its wisdom that builds a house my brother.

<u>Controlling</u>

Definition

- *To direct and exercise authority over someone.*
- *To regulate or hold in constraint physically or mentally*
- *To enforce your will upon another selfishly by force or manipulating*
  Things, factors and situations

Sir Please deal with your insecurities.
We as men have a tendency to exemplify controlling behaviors based on fear of failure, negative thinking/perceptions and past hurts.
Be secure within yourself, a woman loves a confident man that is emotionally balanced and able to handle her without panic when she's in her emotions. Stop manipulating to get your way. This behavior enslaves abuses, divides and is a turn off. We must grow up and be the men God called us to be. Full of faith, prayerful, diligent and of good character.

Vision

Definition

- *The way in which one sees and conceives of something*
- *A image from your creativity, ideal and Ideals*
- *The blue print to a destination*

Scripture says where there's no vision the people perish

Also to write the vision and make it plain so they that read it may run with it. It's very important as a man to have a vision with short term goals attached to it for strategic planning to apprehend a successful future. If you have a family then you must be clear as to where you're leading them to.

You must get before God for clarity, direction and timing.

Communication

Definition

- *The act or process of communicating, Transmission/Commune*
- *The exchange of ideas, messages, mail and information*
- *By speech, signal, telephone and other technology*

Effective communication is what you say, how you say it and with the body language you display while speaking or just as a non verbal expression.

Good connection with your woman and agreement is contingent upon Effective communication. If you don't put in practice the respect of a matured communing then there is no point of business or personal relation established or in order. That goes for with her or other outside relations.

Quality Time

Definition

- *Time in which intimacy is shared that breeds progression and betterment to the relationship Quality Time is the love language of those individuals who grew up with the privilege of someone treating them special by taking them out or being specific in place of fellowship or an intimacy geared toward their liking, So as they have gotten older one way of knowing a person loves them is when they are treated accordingly, when the other person sacrifices time to impart affection and fellowship in their favor.*

  Quality Time is a must for your woman don't let her even get to a point where she has to ask you, unless it's a special engagement date. Speaking of date, Can you say Date Night!? It's mandatory from inception of a relationship throughout its apex and end.

Respect

Definition

- *To feel or show differential regard for*
- *To avoid interference with or violation*
- *To esteem highly and give regard or concern*

You must give respect to get respect.
This is how it's earned.
Learn to Respect others protocol, property, title, space and time.

Respect Order

Manipulation

Definition

- *A devious Management for one's own advantage*
- *Shrewd behavior,*
- *To falsify or tamper with*

God is not pleased with plotting manipulative plans to over through, seize or damage an individual for your personal gain.

Teach your kids to wait on God and opportunity

If you and your significant other put in practice manipulating one another, I think it's time for counseling or closure.

Observation

Definition

- *The act of taking mental or written notation*
- *To record*

Paying close attention to your woman and kids builds trust and strong bonds, because you take great interest in them to meet their needs.

Scripture says to dwell with your with according to knowledge which means you got to pay close attention in order to understand her and the why behind it.

Intercession

- *The entreaty of another by prayer to God on their behalf*

  As a man you are the Priest of your home and your reliance should be in God as him being your total source and resource... Calling on God on behalf of Family and Friends should be done regularly.

Blessed

- *Fortunate than some others, Possessing quality materials, Joyful, Gods presence and favor*

  Teach your kids to count their blessings and to serve and give to the less fortunate.

  Teach them to enjoy and appreciate because tomorrow is not promised

Redeemed

Definition

- *To regain possession of by purchase.*
- *To rescue or ransom, To pay off*

We have been redeemed back to God through the blood of Jesus, the sacrificial lamb that was slain for the sin of mankind.

Concerning Kids

Concerning Kids

- *Provide*

Definition

- *Teach*

Definition - noun
- noun: **teaching**; plural noun: **teachings** the occupation, profession, or work of a teacher. ideas or principles taught by an authority.
- *It is important to be a model for yours kids, to show as an example, integrity, show your children that you can say what you mean and be honest in your daily life and business dealings.*

Scriptures concerning teaching:

- Show yourself in all respects to be a model of good works, and in your teaching show integrity, dignity, and sound speech that cannot be condemned, so that an opponent may be put to shame, having nothing evil to say about us.
- **Proverbs 22:6** ESV / 397 helpful votes
- Train up a child in the way he should go; even when he is old he will not depart from it.
- **James 3:1-2** ESV / 361 helpful votes
- Not many of you should become teachers, my brothers, for you know that we who teach will be judged with greater strictness. For we all stumble in many ways. And if anyone does not stumble in what he says, he is a perfect man, able also to bridle his whole body.
- **Luke 6:40** ESV / 250 helpful votes
- A disciple is not above his teacher, but everyone when he is fully trained will be like his teacher.
- **1 Peter 4:10** ESV / 201 helpful votes
- As each has received a gift, use it to serve one another, as good stewards of God's varied grace:
- **Psalm 32:8** ESV / 164 helpful votes
- I will instruct you and teach you in the way you should go; I will counsel you with my eye upon you.

- **Deuteronomy 32:2** ESV / 148 helpful votes
- May my teaching drop as the rain, my speech distill as the dew, like gentle rain upon the tender grass, and like showers upon the herb.
- **Proverbs 1:1-33** ESV / 106 helpful votes
- The proverbs of Solomon, son of David, king of Israel: To know wisdom and instruction, to understand words of insight, to receive instruction in wise dealing, in righteousness, justice, and equity; to give prudence to the simple, knowledge and discretion to the youth— Let the wise hear and increase in learning, and the one who understands obtain guidance, ...
- **Romans 12:6-7** ESV / 99 helpful votes
- Having gifts that differ according to the grace given to us, let us use them: if prophecy, in proportion to our faith; if service, in our serving; the one who teaches, in his teaching;
- **2 Timothy 2:15** ESV / 82 helpful votes
- Do your best to present yourself to God as one approved, a worker who has no need to be ashamed, rightly handling the word of truth.

- *Inheritance*

  - *Definition* - money, property, etc., that is received from someone when that person dies
  - : something from the past that is still important or valuable
  - : the act of inheriting something

We tend to leave our children what we have accomplished in life, whether it is property, money or something of value. The Bible tells us that we are to leave a legacy for our love ones. This is why is it imperative that we know God's plan for our lives, so that we can receive God's plan and vision for the family. This can be passed on to our great grandchildren and their children as well. The Bible also teaches us about the promised inheritance as well, which is sealed promised Holy Spirit. Study the scriptures below about our promised inheritance.

  - *Scriptures concerning inheritance*

    - **Proverbs 13:22** ESV / 232 helpful votes
    - **A good man leaves an inheritance to his children's children, but the sinner's wealth is laid up for the righteous.**
    - **Epheslans 1:11-14** ESV / 177 helpful votes

- In him we have obtained an inheritance, having been predestined according to the purpose of him who works all things according to the counsel of his will, so that we who were the first to hope in Christ might be to the praise of his glory. In him you also, when you heard the word of truth, the gospel of your salvation, and believed in him, were sealed with the promised Holy Spirit, who is the guarantee of our inheritance until we acquire possession of it, to the praise of his glory.
- **Colossians 3:23-24** ESV / 115 helpful votes
- Whatever you do, work heartily, as for the Lord and not for men, knowing that from the Lord you will receive the inheritance as your reward. You are serving the Lord Christ.
- **Proverbs 20:21** ESV / 113 helpful votes
- An inheritance gained hastily in the beginning will not be blessed in the end.
- **Psalm 37:29** ESV / 72 helpful votes
- The righteous shall inherit the land and dwell upon it forever.
- **Titus 3:7** ESV / 67 helpful votes
- So that being justified by his grace we might become heirs according to the hope of eternal life.
- **Acts 20:32** ESV / 67 helpful votes
- And now I commend you to God and to the word of his grace, which is able to build you up and to give you the inheritance among all those who are sanctified.
- **Ephesians 1:18** ESV / 65 helpful votes
- Having the eyes of your hearts enlightened, that you may know what is the hope to which he has called you, what are the riches of his glorious inheritance in the saints,
- **Galatians 5:19-21** ESV / 65 helpful votes
- Now the works of the flesh are evident: sexual immorality, impurity, sensuality, idolatry, sorcery, enmity, strife, jealousy, fits of anger, rivalries, dissensions, divisions, envy, drunkenness, orgies, and things like these. I warn you, as I warned you before, that those who do such things will not inherit the kingdom of God.
- **Romans 8:17** ESV / 59 helpful votes
- And if children, then heirs—heirs of God and fellow heirs with Christ, provided we suffer with him in order that we may also be glorified with him.

•

- *Training*

Definition

- *Family Time -*
Definition

_____

_____
_____
_____
_____

- *Team*
Definition

_____
_____
_____
_____
_____

- *Bonding*
Definition

_____
_____
_____
_____

- *Confidence*
Definition

_____
_____

_____
_____
_____

- *Peace*

Definition

_____
_____
_____
_____
_____

- *Persistence*

Definition

_____
_____
_____
_____

- *Discipline*

Definition

- *Disciple*

Definition

- *Leadership*

Definition

- *Affirmation*

Definition

- **Affliction**

Definition

- **Righteousness**

Definition

- **War**

Definition

- **Seeds**

Definition

- **Gratitude**

Definition

- **Appreciation**

Definition

- **Sin**

Definition

- **Christian**

Definition

85

- ***Progress***
  Definition

- ***Impact***
  Definition

www.ingramcontent.com/pod-product-compliance
Lightning Source LLC
Chambersburg PA
CBHW031607110426
42742CB00037B/1324